SCHOLASTIC

Let's Find Out

My REBUS Reader

I0890047

Penguins Can't Fly!

by Mark Bailey

SCHOLASTIC INC.
New York Toronto London Auckland Sydney New Delhi Hong Kong

A  can dive.

A  can swim.

penguin

A  can slide.

penguin

Chinstrap Penguin

A  can hop.

penguin

A  can splash.

penguin

A  can waddle.

penguin

King Penguins

A  can go, go, go!

penguin